Of a Feather

Of a Feather

Michael Daley

for Sherry
with thanks +
admiration

Dec 12, '21

Empty Bowl   Port Townsend, 2016

Cover art: John James Audubon: Pileated Woodpecker.
(Commons/ Public Domain)

Set in Minion Pro by Tonya Namura.

Library of Congress Control Number: 2015953165
ISBN 978-0-912887-45-6
Copyright © 2016 by Michael Daley
All Rights Reserved
Empty Bowl Press
A division of Pleasure Boat Studio: A Literary Press
201 West 89th Street, 6F
New York, NY 10024
Tel / Fax: 888-810-5308
www.pleasureboatstudio.com / pleasboat@nyc.rr.com

Acknowledgements

These poems first appeared in the following publications:

"Finding a Way Into" (*Dalmo'ma*, 1976), "Planting Silver Fir above Silver Creek" (*Working the Woods/Working the Sea*, 1984), "On the deck with a cup of coffee, I hear a loud drilling" (*Spillway*, 2015), "Platanus Racemosa" (*Unbroken*, 2015), "Moon has spilled from iced curves" (*Cirque*, 2015), "Gentle Dong" & "The Loss of Beauty" (*Gargoyle #65*, 2016), "When T. McNulty discovered RS's Shack Notebook for March '81" (*Robert Sund Tribute Anthology*, 2016, ed. Piper & Frost).

The author offers his deep gratitude for the support and friendship of many people during the composition of these poems: Mike O'Connor, Finn Wilcox, Jack Estes, Tim McNulty, Sam Green, Larry Laurence, Brad & Boni Killion, Molly McNulty, Steven Dolmatz, Terri Bakke-Shultz, Kathy Prunty, Theo Daley, Eleanor Daley, Maureeen Louzan, Steve & Janet Clark, Bob Rose, Bo Miller, Paul Hansen, Jim Bodeen, Clemens Stark, Paul Hunter, Bill Porter, Frank Moffett and Johnny McDonough.

For Steve Clark

"Nature has looked uncommonly bare & dry to me for a day or two. With our senses applied to the surrounding world we are reading our own physical and corresponding moral revolutions. Nature was so shallow all at once I did not know what had attracted me all my life. I was therefore encouraged when going through a field this evening, I was unexpectedly struck with the beauty of an apple tree—The perception of beauty is a moral test."

—Henry David Thoreau, *Journal 1852*

"Materialism, which is not tainted by ideological abuse of the soul, has a universal and realistic concept of salvation. It admits the reality of Hell only at one definite place, here on earth, and asserts that this Hell was created by Man (and by Nature). Part of the Hell is the ill-treatment of animals—the work of a human society whose rationality is still the irrational."

—Herbert Marcuse, *One Dimensional Man*

TABLE OF CONTENTS

Of a Feather

1.
White rollers on Burrows Bay,
wind in the hemlocks,
coyote scat on the lawn,
I stopped the dog just
before she rolled her neck in it,
to swap scents.
How am I not
the luckiest man?

2.
The deer enter our yard unafraid,
appalled.

My father's car tics
after I dream his journey across America,

where a family whispers,
but the nurses call on us who are white.

Chipped paint on his walls,
Dr. Lynch removed the splinter from my eye.

The deer in the driveway,
his headlight an insult.

Like the eagle near the schoolhouse
two valiant crows rousted out of cedar.

Waves of herons' necks and cat tails
shift, solemn in a breeze.

At my father's deathbed, the man in a white cloak
climbed a ladder.

The little apples clump,
soft-voiced deer return to them in evening light.

At sunset,
the core of gold in my fist.

3.
Moon has spilled from iced curves,
thermostat busted, house chilled.

In warm sleep
you spoon my scrawny shank,
I know your perfect fire.

So long ago
your heat consumed me, illumined
years,
their nights still clanking.

From the triangular skylight
and across our hips,
overlapped
beneath the roiling quilt,
drops
a folded napkin of moon.

4.
The meadow sunset climbs the deck,
then tips all our roofs across the gully.
No one raking, one busy swallow sails
in and out the shade, acre-thick alder
obscure our million-dollar view.
Downhill, sight of the rocky shore's vanished,
though our window faces where it used to be
after a forest, tall as stacks of houses, fell to saws
under glass now in the county museum,
and gave us this view of sunset
rippling the top of Mt. Erie.

5.
Haven't you seen
the frog's silhouette?
How, beside the puddle,
he looks like a hairless old man
crouched to escape my hand
stretched out with best intentions?
I'm a blond child frog-hunting
while you, my adult at the wheel,
wouldn't squash a frog
or creep your tire forward
till I've rescued it—
though you'll have to wait,
tired and cold, just beyond
the dome of our house
all the while I claw my way back up the gully,
or I could start from here
in your headlights
chasing the tree frog away from the cliff edge,

my stagger something like a hop,
while my white hair flops in the rain.

6.
Across the lake in the darkness
is a light where a man sits at a table
eating a breakfast of oatmeal
and writing his first poem of the day.
When he looks into darkness
he knows the giant cedar is out there,
and the lake—last night a tub of dull moon—
hasn't dried up, or changed
in any way apparent or important.
He sees one light, only this one,
where someone at a kitchen table
(with oatmeal, and scribbling)
doesn't trouble what lies
in the dark between us.

7.
The afternoon with paired ruby-throated hummingbirds,
two robins—one sails in, one away, a tag team—
a stream of worms yanked alive from uncut buttercups
into three gape-mouthed hatchlings,
the gold Persian chattering at the windowsill.
Now we're all worn out.

8.
On the deck with a cup of coffee, I hear a loud drilling
into what must be the cedar beside the driveway
and not the maple where I would have seen
that powerhouse who's making the racket, while almost
in response there's another driller from across the wide gully.

A call and response between two giant woodpeckers,
possibly three. Pilleated—by how loud they are.
An odd sensation that the work they do—
and not only them: there are the silent ants,
and sow bugs through the sand—is a
dismantling, splinter by grain by rain droplet,
of this entire valley, that Mt. Erie in the distance
would be shown through time-lapse photographs
to disintegrate thanks to the blind industriousness
in those seriously determined ruby-headed managers
whose well-paid employees snarfle in the duff.

9.
On loving talons
the eagle points the mole
to where cattails divide swamp from clear-cut,
napalm-blackened, a shined-by-rain plastic gas can
on a stump—a blind mess in wet fir,
white forepaws in mid-leap beyond control.

10.
The bee caught in rhododendron
tightens as it twirls
in the strands of a spider's web,
until its soft form goes limp
and quits its kicking.
Then a brother bee
zings under branches,
snips the snare
and both tear away
from purple blossoms.

11.
You bring it back,
the way your hands rise up and clench,
tease yourself all over again,
a smoke billowing off your fist,
long hair blowing
as you stagger Maclean Road's frost,
traffic, a herd aware an instant only
of you: angry, redhead, drunk.

12.
Back through all those damages I soared
through memory and thunder, and plummeted
onto a trail etched disastrously out of earth
by something wild and akin to me who drinks
now and then some blue from the sky
only to fall helplessly into arms of steel
across the winding dogged river
I still love, torn loose from it
by uselessness, and from myself.

13.
First light scoops
a crystal chip
out of the lake,
billows the shape of a small town
drift off a burnt stump.
If I needed to change my life,
that'd be my perch, in the glare.
The heron high steps,
her neck almost bearable—
and, hunched shade,
she thrusts her beak.

I have to look away
when she throws open
her wild winged smock.

14.
On the Keystone Ferry,
a straw broom and dust pan
left near my seat,
I pick them up, and get to work.

15.
Slightly drunk on the ferry,
he overhears Polish.
They tell him where they're from.
He advises places to tour.
"Don't tell anyone
you're from France," whispering
—they have banded against xenophobes.
"But we're not from France!"
Their voices thin waves against the hull.
"Don't tell Americans. Know why?
'What's it like in Paris?'
'Did you sample our wine?
Can you stomach the food here?'"
"We're not from France."
"That's right.
Tell them that.
"Je suis Quebecois!"
Smiles at them, lifts his graffittied
duffle bag to a shoulder,
all but doffs his cap,
walks off, stops, one finger up:
stage whisper, *"Vive La France!"*

16.
One strawberry
falls over the lip of the bowl,
flips once,
then again—to the edge of the counter
where the soft roll
stops
on its triangular nub, a last
kernel failing
to gain purchase,
wobbles, forgotten
till three of her fingers
whisk it,
her wrist revolves it,
without thought, she scoops it—a ripe
strawberry—
to her lips.

17.
Just as I turn out the light,
the curtain fills with the spring of 1962—
that small blue smell
of suddenly open seeds spread over the car
conjured my white fist of a face
to leer from the attic window,
fifteen year old teeth,
shock of lightning hair,
radio gloomy
as The Rondelles met The Stones.
I climbed over the back porch rail
with a muddy pack crammed
with rocks and books and quahog shells

from my mucky pearl
of bold Nantasket Beach.

18.
The rose enters the sky at dawn,
clouds shed ghosts,
waves safe on the long beach of ballet
blushing to a pebble.
A gold shaft in Boston Light
dwindles on the horizon.
Half the moon, a row of polished stone,
assorted chips of colored glass, a gull,
a foot pressed sixty years ago, and
a girl afraid to swim, a striped ball,
no trace of me, but the same waif
dawdles on the sand.

19.
Willa likes to chew her tennis ball
until the hide drops off
so both halves in my hand
put me back on Annabel Street,
Dorchester, half-ball with a broomstick:
Home the broken pit repaved
to the lumpy middle of the street,
First a *Desoto's* chrome bumper,
Second the Fire Station hose,
Third splinters from the telephone pole
ripped by Hurricane Carol.
Mostly pimple balls someone with a blade
probably the twins' brother Bobby
had to slice in two

so if you wrapped your index
and fuck-you fingers round
always curved across home plate
and might've got to outfield
but you had to really whack it
for homeruns onto Mary Anderson's steps
and I get through six quick innings
with Billy Boni, The Shadhouser
and Jimmy & Johnny before
she needs to fetch her half a ball
across the lawn again.

20.
Dog in the yard: rabbit's mind's
bumping down the hill,
quail with speckled offspring
buzz the pavement,
go invisible into tall weeds,
so do the doe—leaping hind
parts sprung, wild ballerinas
in a daisy meadow.

21.
Not far, the horse whinnies,
a nasal whistle, exalted and un-
mistakable, and she neighs,
insistent, giving morning birdsong
the confidence
of her tail's sweep.

22.
Till this trill
of Vivaldi's *Piccolo Concerto*,
I heard nothing.

Voices never spoke, storm winds
had been drone,
birdsong
static.

My ears reborn, the piccolo
jigs a brisk sunlight
onto the hood of my car.

Stoplight, exhaust smoke,
the lace of poplar's merry arms
against an azure frozen January—all
sway to tones
absolute
as icebergs were once.

Then the light changes.
Together in sweats, identical earbuds,
two strollers chatter through their shy beauty,
cross to a riff of pedestrian flautinos
driving sunlight up a wheel rim,
the afternoon a drowsy dog.

But inside the streaks of shade,
a hooded woman on the sidewalk,
scarved and gloved,

her face cracked by the crinkled bright air,
mouth cringed inward,
despairs
of her course, and runs,
stealing all the sunlight,
a cloud bassooning after her,
shrill arpeggios trailing.

And now we can never recover.
No instrument exists on earth
to rescue us.

23.
The birdfeeder catches the last streak of light,
reflecting it into the house, and seems to play—
like that kid with a magnifying glass
who shot a sharp beam till you caught him.
Sundown pierces the window and also
the silver-spotted body of a blown-glass bird
who always rests on the windowsill, silent.
Redwings off the marsh, juncos, yellow-patterned
grosbeaks rock so their frenzy spilling seed
sets the feeder to its rhythmic shine
in my eye again, till the sun passes our roof,
random shade running off, with a wink.

24.
Two ravens approach the lake from the north ridge.
Their uttered vows draw us from garden lettuce
and handicapped carrots the sweat in soil bred.
Then quiet. Not a wheel reels south,
the party in the hills naps, that voice
I've known every year of adulthood, that rasp,

barroom, prison-smoked drawl beaten from birth,
crisp, and innocent of despair, gone quiet.
Except the whip of daylight wings black as love
high over a reddened alder grove,
I hear only the throb inside my mind.

25
Two chickadees,
      black caps sprinkled
              by this morning's shower,
bend slender roses
      where a drunk bee
         clings undisturbed
by the hummingbird's
      thunderous needle bill
         as the chickadees nibble
microscopic mites
      off rose leaves'
         underbellies.

26.
First sun strikes the wet bare field we love,
I mutter under sword fern how thoughtlessly
horsetails resprout by leaf rot, nudge sow beetles,
plume clots of dung crisp soils.
Then waddle over the hot pavement
like a salamander, ignoring any reason
not to lounge in the lawn chair, reading poetry,
recovering, I'll say, should anyone notice
weeds spool laughably under my Japanese Maple,
from an ache I can't name the muscle for,
where aches go deep to the heart, barely aware
of the distant tender pulse of a dove.

27.
In its last brush stroke,
an hour's perfection
leaves almost enough ink
for the stately flotation
of a nail paring too little
to call Moon,
black become blue smudge,
these minutes when nothing
significant happens.

28.
The sun with quiet authorial indifference
publishes a new poem
on leaves of willow and maple,
fronds of yew and cedar,
as a blond blue-veined knee of madrona
sways always east. Slowly. Slowly.

No one has ambition
who knows what reckless metaphor
the blue sky hides.
No one sees its grandeur
erase lesser poets' night mistakes,
or put out all our lights.

29.
Snow geese squawk,
        Sunday morning,
                in waves and veils,
circle the barns,
        rust drips from a nail,

                    gray cloud towers
streaked from bouquets
                    of rising sun.

My window down,
            engine quiet,
                        my God,
what a racket
            across Fir Island.
What a shimmer
            their swinging arrows
                        across my face.

Six Haibun

New England Hawks in October

On a windy day here in Hull, a small hawk perched on the seawall, and because it watched me coming close, I thought it was injured, or even poisoned. I approached slowly, its head turned toward me, eyes clicking on my every move. Eyes of a predator—that hawk studied me with patience and eagerness. When I held out a stick to see if it would take hold, it stepped back, the sharp eyes focused on me. Three feet away. It was then I realized those talons might rip off my face and that pale green beak could grind my eyeball. I stepped over the seawall where whitecaps barreled from Boston Light. When I turned again, the hawk was in flight, wide wingspan coasting over sailboats at anchor. It appeared to be a Kestrel, or a Sparrow Hawk, clinging to a concrete seawall. Heavy wind. A few days before, a much larger hawk, a Red Tail, clung to the verdigris spire of the Greek Orthodox church beside my sister's house, its mate most probably nesting in the woodlot across the street. Yesterday evening a Swainson's hawk alighted on the dead branch of an elm in the yard. I'd been reading Thoreau's *Cape Cod Journal*, and remembered it starts right here, weathering the wild; that is, he came through Hull, and then caught up with a shipwreck in Cohasset, Irish immigrant corpses all along the stormy beach. Our house was once a railway stop. In my imagination, old Henry David trudges up the hillside to start his long trek down the Cape. I'd like to be a good observer, and learn from his books, but when I see this hawk, I can't help myself, and my three steps across the grass are enough for it to drop down and swoop across our little avenue, where it hides now, for all I know, in the neighbor's tall hedges, already enflamed as the famous trees here do these crisp weeks.

Why write? Why else each day
does the hawk fall
to its fierce grass,
a clear and sullen line,
talons stabbing once
aim true as desire?

Gentle Dong

It's not what you think. Ushered through velvet, its name
over a door whose veiled origins hum, those wounded
by the strange device entered a hall swimming in light.
Beloveds hinting dispossession, whole countries of regret
mapped on faces, bridges to our sullen art. An old man
delights in readiness, while women joked, "How do you go
around wearing one of those?" Happy weapon, it wakes us
mid-dream to worry the prostate, embarrasses at school
board meetings; caffeine affected, it drips in the rush. In
a cumbersome codpiece, pissing wars in the later years,
this contraption, or one like it never much improved
upon, fueled history, led assault, swung the club, brokered
the treaty, broke it, planted starts for endless replication,
and can't be blamed. Soft tissue one's hand might brush
tossing in insomnia and be reminded of another's touch.
Nurse changing linen so casually comes close as if it were
kneecap, big toe, a pretty piece of flesh, a dingle's lightning
rod, wishbone off the fault line. Phenomenon we perish
by, a high percentage do, or ignore at our peril that grave-
pointing finger, water witch, proboscis of delusion we so
charmingly hide.

> Princely Hummingbird
> sliver tip, narwhal-like,
> vanishes in northern azure,
> throbs on a wire
> above his domain of roses.

Taking the Scent

Too much bourbon and I blasted Raul sitting beside the lovely Thalia, for suggesting I should think of the planet as a speck of dirt afloat in space. He didn't mean "worthless," but perhaps "temporary," and smacked of Jesuit school preference for afterlife. Yesterday, selecting new glasses, I saw consumption as the bite of inevitability—how long till I won't need these? Timelessness in an operational world is for monks and hermits. To obsess over "life span" marginalizes me. Starlight travels billions of years, but "travel" is not exactly real. The metaphor helps me comprehend light by using an eye as a destination. When I've wondered why so-called great figures concerned themselves with what happened after their deaths, I've missed seeing they understood inevitability. Not only from religious beliefs in an afterlife—even strict atheists address issues to be resolved, if resolved, after their deaths. To see beyond a throwaway world, to not think I am replaceable, or on a journey. Until recently, hardly a church made earth its business—stewardship a poorly derived Biblical term like dominion—and not an afterthought or obligation whereas love of place is the persuasion of timelessness.

> The tip of my pen
> noses this white,
> in shadows scrolls
> the map to mortality.

The Loss of Beauty

The way a face haunts us with its purity about the lips, within the eyes' glow, its frank pleasure in being; we can't exhaust ourselves with looking. All day every face gives everything it has to offer in the briefest encounters, but we need to see this one face perform. More than stillness, the eye needs its laughter, its calm trust, even savagery if we can withstand a sudden loss in one face out of millions.

> We cannot survive.
> Hearts roam continents panting
> over the wooden road.

PLATANUS RACEMOSA

When the tree in its bones begins to green, bud to early leaf, an aura enlivens, and dormancy gets involved with breeze, the rain and light. Suddenly birds not seen in these parts for some time take to it, a squirrel begins to hide. Yet, beside the gym, intricacy of branching twists a budding sycamore. The bark, peeling and pale, is the face of John Ruskin and his motley beard. Its branches draw figures against the lightening sky; it's hard not to feel consumed. We walk past these artists, themselves their own creation, collaborators with sun and rain, soil and fertilizer, preoccupied with our own branching of thought, the pace of our walk, serenity or a lack thereof playing at our lips. I think of my student's face texting a friend as she worked her way upstairs. Such peace emerges with all else let go: doubts and fog and protestation, judgment, grudges, and accumulated sleights. My unworthiness. As if my presence mattered, as if I'm imbued with secret knowledge.

> Cleansed of grief
> under waking sycamore
> mad clouds bloom.

Evening in Port Townsend, 1977

I'm in a box—you can't even tell what's in it—heaved up by
two centuries of bricklayers—except for the lives gone past
like jeweled glitter in the marina at the tips of creaking
masts, the brindled deck rails of yachts, berthed and
canopied under the galaxy with its unthinkable black hole.
Mountains unfold and fold again, dimpled unwavering
snow light and grades of gray, of blue; the Mill's white fluff
butters the air, sandy bluffs fade and tilt backward from
the sun, TV antennae and prongs of hemlock up where
houses picket the skyline. Pilings dot the muck. Gull-
stolen and parchment-thin crab hovels whistling sea air,
cracked on rocks and surface water, smear low tide. The
Ferry, a passage of spirits entranced on engine throb,
distant ghost islands in the mist, white pocked houses
and cupolas, and the day's light—at 7.53—going down,
is a long strip of vanilla-yellow, jiggy over the slightest of
waves. One sailboat, mainsail luffing, another becalmed,
shadows throughout town flow up the bluffs and rise into
the streets, Morgan Hill a cap of fir spikes. Old aghast
buildings, mortar fragile as paper, a paper town, the
hundreds of windows bright lit and going dark on all the
third, fourth and fifth floors where secrets I know and
you don't reek like a drunk forgetting and reshaping what
happened before today, which is nothing new, although
the sun might pass over the Cascades only one more time.

Parking lot lights go on.

Equinox Eve

1.

A white sail cups its ear for breeze enough to listen
all the way across the blue calm surface of the song
sea spread today over airways chill and paradisal,
song of the evening glowing, like a candle sputters,
a last full day of winter, eve of equinox
pleasant for the crocus emanating safely enough,
horsetails charging down the gully, not a frost in sight,
but an hour to the south snowballs of ice,
peppered the sidewalk, belting sprouted daffodils,
popping off helmets of giggling bicyclists,
chasing a suspicion of crows away from the wake of one,
who, ennobled by injury, didn't make it into spring.

2.

Elephant ears
I slip under,
skunk cabbage,
the stream noisy
as it drops
into mud, and I breathe
through a reed.
I am commando.
Captain Bullfrog
pulling my way
through watery
cabbage roots
to where is that
croaking
and I come up

beside huge bright
yellow balls,
green phallus,
scent that lifted
tail of a skunk
blossoms
in wild leaves, ears
who love this
music frogs perform.
I could drift for acres
in this gold swamp,
its light swims
heaven's sump
and only frogs
to celebrate.
Oh let me, let
me in where
the stream sings
its yellow throbbing
into the clit
of leaf, ears
too big
to hear
my croak,
or song.

3.
I'm that frog in a field of frogs,
a wild note under the new moon
in swamp and slug rain,
a castanet deep in the throat,
by creek high on mud sluiced

through cattle dung—
that fool, that bellows of devotion
in blood and breath,
passionate amphibian
on creaky thigh bones.
I give up my heart to sing.
I am that *tharumph* of frog,
my wet legs springing to song.

4.
Eleven
times the
dark
chipmunk
scurls
the twisted
bark of
maple—
goes around
to go up—
eleven
circles
the dogs
whip
round the
trunk and
bark.

5.
Pillbox, lid dented, thumbed
in my black pocket, coin-rubbed
so the tin shines through—

faded paint of a lupine:
a mountain river scene. In my palm
this box, heft of a hummingbird,

held my sister's pills which grew
too many. Now its gold inner foil
crowns my own week of white tablets.

Seven moons flood my bloodstream,
ride the ridges of seven
days I scrawled: S, M, T, W, and so—

my box of immortality,
every day eternal mountain rivers
rage in me forever.

6.
That ruby on the knobbed hood
of that woodpecker, careworn, at the feeder;
glitter in turquoise along the throat of Anna's
hummingbird, released last week after a crash,
from my 'clinic,' a cardboard box
punched for air and eucalyptus;
so deep a red, nearly purple,
the rough nose of thimbleberry
growing mold so far north;
also, that smooth sleek tan
trembling hide of the deer
picking her stealthy way, exposed
all up the rock garden;
and white swells mounting twenty feet
of lost rock-faces spray the beach,
this week's storm across Burrows Bay

swept away then back again against
a dangerous tilting maple;
and, odd, the deep brown
tail feathers and gnarled beak
of the Peregrine, a little arrogant
glaring off our deck—at us
too awed to leave the car;
then my shock in cardboard
at how orange, and beige,
the rigid thrush, the hawk's hit
we'd argued how to save, a thing
we can't unlearn, like song.

7.
Body of a finch,
gold, or yellow really, like something
store-boughten
as they say up-river,
colored by
            no pretty little hand
in the Philippines
with a brush and wistful smile
across its breast feathers,
                        curved talons larger
than you thought they'd be,
the whole bird in fact
                        large, not the tiny flash
you once felt so lucky
to catch a glimpse of, but hefty,
a plump one with its few flies,
slow and reverent, who attend
        the sublime
sleeper—that's a kindness to say—

golden eyes wide open
          an omen some would believe,
whether of ill luck or a new day
here on the rocks
in crisp sun
below your window.

Fall Notebook

September 12
The sea was in its glass, my
mind in a cup brewing as
a wave uncurled on sand seeped
into cool tide pools. This thought
minces on gravel with that—
this thought, that thought—this and that.
A dot-dot, Dadaist itch
for the sea, the sea comes back
drenched in love, a thing I wish
I'd said to warn the county.

September 24
Awake to find numbers reeling
in the teacup, a science of
possibilities comingling
but why my dragon-mouthed teacup?

Doctors creep in constant pursuit,
rationalize the dark dawn,
never surprised (I can't leap but
watch me fly,

                work my way around
this cliff face), who, when they catch me,
say, 'We'll only need a sample
of your blood, just for the record.'

September 25
No matter the weather,
yellow leaves of alder,

and broadleaf maple will
certainly tumble to
the grass, but baritone
wind chimes, long steel, clang once
so we know—as branches
in our orchards appear
bare when the small fingers
of piece workers rush through
their limbs, so does chaos
pluck the color from apples
and leave only chewed stems.

September 29
If you count hairs on a head,
stars, sand, all inhales, exhales
we mammals have yet to take,
where are we? Dire predictions
unite us: hit by a rock,
tsunami, calm breath never
heard again, no posturing
for newspapers, no other
news. What stays new? Only the
mind extolling limitless
shadows across sundials,
the hourglass sand, and bald stars.

September 30
Hummingbird in October.
We keep the feeder full, its
vial drips alone until
the next approach to tap a
bit from the plastic rose—the
last, moments ago, were buds.

Now they're disappointments, it
seems to me, who could refill
my soul with sugar, and feed
this lit trembling lingerer.

October 1
Hayden Carruth has died and I noticed
in reading his *Collected* the use of
syllabics would cause a line to split a-
poetically we might say or at least
against the grain. If a poem can be said,
it can be said to have a grain, a nat-
ural way within the love of word for
word or for phoneme that rubs us all wrong
if the language tries to jerk us all a—
round. Carruth, though, didn't really do that.

October 3
Brants soon will cut across our sturdier
trees and we'll lift our eyes from the nest of
garden hose or the last mowing, a rake,
to hear the sound of wings, a canvas flap
in a sullen squall, and throaty sadness.
Forty years ago, the loose shape of mouths,
a foul dawn about to dive to new depths
beneath the fleets of trawling cloud, gray mugs,
coffee and cigarettes at the café,
a bitter fisherman alluded to
the owner what he'd like to do with his,
the owner's, wife, a thin silent woman
from Vietnam. The grim offensive
arises on every front. All
winter it may go this way: something

like a smile, polite service that sour fuck
never deserved, all through the rain panting
in every street, patterns imitated
by the meticulous artist also
at the counter, who, when he threw his brush,
said he could connect the generations
to love, even love complaints of the Brants,
for instance, who give us a voice for ours
for shredded iron clouds we're sailing to
on heliotrope evenings, for skewed light.

October 7
The rain last night as cruel
as the biblical god, and
then it's over. A flood and
then becalmed, kayaks checking
on the neighbors. Hurricanes,
killer wind, wrecked lives, traffic
panic to flee and then we
count the dead, sigh to be alive.
The storm and aftermath, waves
of circumstance, an orange
peel's hooked shape. Life of danger,
days of comfort.

October 8
At a distance a semi
creeps around the winding ridge,
driver wide awake, no use
resenting these hairpin turns
up in the air, no feeling
at the low gear required.
All cargo precious, one who

steers that vehicle, fearless,
through the eye of a needle
knows why.

Oct 10

      May the deep ink slip
along a surface like an
ice skater from Canada
with years of experience,
polite monk who knows better
than let his enthusiasms
direct his spiritual life,
figure eights for god.

Oct 13

                    Who says
so but the clock stripped bare of
authority? Mirrors droop,
the cat looks on with little
expectation, leaves sprinkle
the new lawn but don't mean to.
Only the second hand, a
broom for spilled sand, gets it right,
says "go" and you do, "do" and
you wish you did.

Oct 15

             The day has
begun, a stillness with gray.
Seated squarely on soft earth,
he talks on—a mole emerged
under the single song of
an elk. With prayers, roses,

colloquies, he sifts a dream,
language for blackberries' root-
ball where whole cities climb out.

Oct 20 St Jerome
The first problem is to illuminate
the letters calligraphed on the granite.
I have been in this cave for 16 days
and I'm past panic, have got a slight wheeze,
and am worried; too old for survival
tactics—to grub for ants, or to col-
lect water from leaves, but contemplative
by nature, I'll decipher walls for half
the day and then watch mountains grow foolish,
and mirror my mind, which too shall perish.

Oct 21
Oh Onion, renowned blossomy mirror,
to the extent the dark machinery
of rib cage and lung ripple like water
when I approach the bank to the flurry
panicky ducks erupt, so do you make
a sane heedless man sloppily to weep
over your slicings, as if to mimic
a feeling: that gypsy outside a shop
in Budapest, drunk, begging, in tears
suddenly, to tell how many are dead,
vagrant and alone, to unravel
his little mystery. He's decided
you peel away and peel away and cry
till the onion's core, love you can't reject.

November 22–23
We watch the flight of two slow snow geese
across a white sky, but from the car
floating the thicker traffic, we wheeze
no more than 'oh' behind the windshield.
Is it just human to hardly note
they're passing, or enlightened to sight,
and count, the snow geese, to call beauty
down upon our engines crawling
to stoplight and free right? The flap of
two white sets of wings loud enough to
stir the mind, the driver's "distracted
from distraction by distraction"—mind
full: radio squawk, hucksters for war,
bald announcers at the wrestling match,
the body's contorted assemblage
in fits and starts, fevered dances of
escape to overcome the dry bones.

St. Desire

1. *"...and wild desire fall like black lightning"*
                              —Ezra Pound

As the salamander's
keeping time
to sod and grist,
deaf to whistles
of redwing, and knock
of the woodpecker
at the drill hole snag,
and to breath,
seed snap under
foot, paw, or the talon
on wind—curt
logic knocking
at the door
with Brother Termite.

2.
Finding a way into,
gray glow
leads down dawn.

Crow carries a rose
to the ground.

First motors
and the old ways
darken in the palm.

The moon, a small foot,
steps into snow.

3.
Alarmed
at a hair
in my oatmeal
(not mine
by its luster),
I spare myself
disgust such
intimacy
causes
as a princess
so pure
and washed
comes to mind
when I, blind
to fearless
microorganisms,
wolf
my porridge.

4.
An icicle under our eaves,
thick tangled fingers point,
two or three melt.

Tracks after half a day:
the dog dragged his hind leg
whimpering over a drift.

On the creases of my palm
moons emerge and melt,
true worlds, cold birds.

The lake still pale,
a string of crisp red Christmas lights
off and on, and off: gray first light—

The lake has the sky's skill
to carry snow
and tease with blue.

Golden in piled cumulus,
sunrise ripples the fir branch,
and we lean on our shovels.

6.
Planting Silver Fir above Silver Creek,
the ground has broken out in stone.
Boulders lie crooked and cracked
in the basin at the creek.
Their formation spells the word
we must never speak.
Glacier water, ice white, falls
and in incessant sighs
runs the slipping ledges
past crackling runt rocks,
soft firemoss, red, and orange.
The water's is the only sound
unless our tools sing metal to the ground.
Then work stops. The snow gossips
for a minute with our clothes.
This high, money should be pebbles in the boot.

But it's not. We count the hours
till we drive down four thousand feet of cloud
to a wave battering
under our beds—how I long to dream
again, but we have work to do. We dig again
in something that has made us. We curse it.
A buzzard's shadow hums in brief sun and we go on.
We do this in the tracks of deer.

7.
Blood moon, and I missed the lunar eclipse.
This feeling I've known only from a poem
about to take place,
undisturbed by my usual fury,
a feeling I locate,
though I can't describe, a taste
metaphorically arisen in my throat,
deeper: I've made a meal out of poetry.

(An old girl-friend claimed she knew me so well
she could see in my eyes
when I was about to write a poem,
but she was mistaken,
they don't hide in the open.)

For three nights this familiar presence,
known to me as Paraclete
under Orion's Belt, as genius,
inhabited black space behind Seven Sisters.
Yet here I stand in the dark
with my wife whom I love
and we kick an orange ball
for a silly dog,

the poem in my quiver
shot to stars
with our rituals toward sleep.

What brought me to draw up
out of drowsy chemistry,
a taste for golden poetry?
What vanity put a scribble to this page?
Doubtless I'm the ape chained to a desk,
coaxed to artistry,
come to darken our murmuring planet,
guided by an incompletion in the stars.

8. *"On The Surface of a Stream*
    into Which a Stone Has Been Cast"
                              —Coleridge

In the six thousand some odd days and nights
we've moved and breathed and had our being
in this dark house, how many sunsets
have we shifted our chairs and strained to watch
in the eastern windows, how many frogs
have come and gone? How many snakes
writhed beneath the trunk of rotting alder?
We are moving to a new place,
but how many currants bloomed and fell?
How many cattails over the swamp?
We have to get down on our knees
and kiss the dirt. Only then can we
saunter off to Kubla's Pleasure Dome.

9. *"...but all places, even those we treasure most are but*
    points on a continuum, brief moments in the passage
    of time through a changing landscape."
                                            —Tim McNulty

The way sunrise
fills the fogbank
and both dissolve,
the way my glass teapot
bells the light,
the way each grass stem
tips a bead of dew—
that's how I choose
when nothing's left—
temporal heat
the world burns up
as it burns.

10. *When T. McNulty discovered RS's Shack Notebook for*
    March '81

The poet Robert Sund
        looks out from his shack
                in time to see
old friend Clyde dock the rowing dory
and plunge
                to his knees
in low tide
        hoisting aloft
                a trophy bottle of Sake.
A mound with trillium trumpets
        above the mud.
Think of Tu Fu and Li Po

who in by now rare incarnations
question is what they invite poetry.

Here we are, Clyde says,
        at the beginning of style.

On a column of trochees
        the archivist scrolled
                to an *"Imagined Marriage"*
no one had seen,
none been told:
                Trillium Lilly
and—*Lilly/ Lilly/ Lilly/ Lilly*
        —more,
                a field all down one page.

Alone by kerosene flicker
solitaries put Fish Town on the map
with calligraphed lists to loves
        unreciprocated
      while the romance of citizens
           barreled along at Pike Place heedless
of Lilly's accordion wheeze and moan
        in sunshine cold
           in gold oblivion streets.
                (for Georgia Johnson)

11.
Mating Dragonflies,
like refueling aircraft,
lift off tall stems,
his majesty's peerless wing
feathers the pup's snout.

12. *"A Butterfly*
    poised on a tender orchid
    how sweetly the incense
    burns on its wings"

                                    —Basho

The Skagit rises
and all the snows of winter
soak down to the corn.

                    •

Rain all day, wind, cats
impatient before dinner,
then frogs. I mean Frogs!

                    •

Skunk almost entered
the school, her carcass scented
the street for three days.

                    •

Wind in the cedars,
only a giant
pirouettes so quietly.

                    •

The moon on my hand
halfway down the ladder
winks in shifting cloud.

                    •

Blown past cedar tips,
two snow geese, white necks stretched, drift
then adjust for wind.

                    •

I follow like deer the way of least resistance
where wave, wind, geese sail.

•

Leaning skis against Juniper pine.
Gray jays
stole my lunch.

•

All these bare maples
perched with hawks
who soon the leaves will hide.

•

The moon drops a crumb
on our snow, and we take
a deep light bath.

•

All the streets rolling
past their dogwood at sunset
footloose to the sea.

•

I wake in the loft.
Was it footsteps on the roof?
Spring is rain walking.

13.
A wasp
at least
awakes
from slumber
with
enough
tired venom
to drop it
on gravel
from
a wineglass.

A man
with a jug
near the gas pump
who wouldn't
take a dollar
shuffles
on hot asphalt,
calls me
gentleman, scholar.

Seven jugs full,
his rusted van
slips past
city limits.

Yogi's
throaty purr
beside our jackets
draped
from a chair
protecting
a mole
who splays
fluffy legs
on polished oak.

Savior once
already today,
I tote him
or her in Tupperware,
blind to the weeds.

Held a hummingbird
in my fingers—
shot from touch
to the last
instant
of dusk
where cedars whip,
and her mate
whirred, then
they beamed
away.

15.
Since I've lived most winters under northern rain,
my boots often stuck in bog soft lawn
pecking my way to the firewood,
on this vacation, what I like best
is to sink into pearl Miami night,
my feet washed and foamed in wave on wave,
tide risen through iambic thuds.
In daylight it's a slower drumming, then silence.
I count the waves to the beat of a waltz, take my pulse
which doesn't dance but whirs by comparison—
throat of a hummingbird against the breath of sea.
Certainly the myths were never far
from vast immeasurable chaos outrageous
as ocean, dark, wasteful, wild entities
breathing behind form, crests in the dark,
wind-fisted white beard rabbis who plough the sand.
A convert to history, I shoulder my oar with them
and march the boardwalk for peace into Gaza.
Or with the old memory men from Havana,
I plot the afterlife beside the parked sedans,

thumb to throat, systole, diastole—the sum
of these beats, my unanticipated life,
lies within a breath of the sea.

16.
I've always been alarmed
by a poet whose confidence
creates the public atmosphere
helping us forget the fist
hammering at the door.

But not Auden.
His fearful cowed body
stooped much larger
than any room back then
needed to be stooped for.

Something black was
hanging from the ceiling, or
from some ceiling.
September, 1939, was there
to rob our eyes
of pleasure in his aged ambiguity.

A poet in blue slippers.
I heard him read,
"We must love one another or die."
Though he disowned the line,
he'd never remove a crackling rebuke to Empire.

Boston College, 1972

17.
Run a little language through the fingers,
squeeze it with teeth cleaned by weeping,
put it down in plain ink.

The concrete slab lies in the sun,
burnt roughed surface
printed by leaves.

Like all saying formed by geometries of blossom,
truth is unpetalled, bare
aggregate rock.

Like the arcing self, grand monkey made in likeness:
I over I, am who am on mountain peaks,
heaven chatter fallen quiet.

18.
In the morning, blood on the bath rug
unexplained.

As night begins, wind scares up excitement
with the boughs and leaves.

The moment passes—jagged hours piercing winter grass—
we fix what age forgives.

In public places, strangers utter revelation unashamed,
a heart on a loosened hinge.

Squalor appears as another's life, our house in the road.
One wrong turn and the party drives in.

No life so exposed gets in its way. Wind picks up,
so many leaves clog the sewer.

19.
My legacy was hip pain and fidelity,
the pin in his I run from—
Zeno's silly arrow
still slipping through the layers
of sleep time, genetic
decades, granite—till,
mid-stride across the parking lot,
I am his bull's eye:

a twang in my atrium,
his rhythm,
goes off between a dream
and the car door,
while my bloodline,
that space-age tribe, recoils.

His become mine, the years alone—
brutal honest years in drafty rooms—
abandoned libido, his cancer crawls
toward my cells. His last hours:
demands, disbelief, visions,
a life he craved, and gone.

Rescue me, delirious Believer,
outstretched on the hospital bed.
Within the destined heart,
dawn's the gown of chance.

The Resurrection of Mole

"Vanitas vanitatum et omia vanitas"

—Ecclesiastes 1:2

1.
The path to Pilchuk's Tree-farm
loops
under tilting alder.
Heavy with summer rains, they bow,
and I slog
through their tunnel.
Upright a decade or two, some lean
beribboned to be dropped.

Scrinched stumps could mean
the sawyer fretted his father
lives alone,
and made his cut too steep
as he gauged both
were out of practice talking.

Fresh-down alder
dot our hills in orange rings.
From a fall, behind a sword fern
or big-eared skunk cabbage,
awkwardly arise
wings spread, white tail feathers
awakened, to scavenge.
Imagine: Giants
raid
your burrow.

2.
Mole is a force
larger than obliteration.
Flapping, the eagle
       in ascent
             with mole,
fantail
uncoils over the log road.

Mole surrenders to the sky.
Ferns twinge,
Mole, on a talon,
takes to the air,
first time ever.

3.
Where swamp water crackles out cat tails,
pioneers
who wandered off trail,
salmonberry, red and gold as caviar,
delectable egg, arc
over grizzled nettles,
green veil dusts the swamp.

Eagle and mole, they twirl on high,
chased by territorial
crow,
who croak from tipping maples
speckled with lichen,
gloved in moss.

Mole sails over the brook beavers worked,
a groove vanished

in the leaf of the County.
Veers
over cut acres,
soot-blackened stumps,
all the way to the quiet neighbors. O
Pioneers! When you pave here,
when you drop
the measure of surveyor chalk,
when you draw up the plans, haul
the slash, pulverize glacial stones,
arise
some summer morning,
tools of misery and consolation,
fearless to the touch
of a match, or fault line, river rise,
but turn like Lot's wife,
and you're salt lick
for the fawn
from the abandoned clear-cut.

4.
I hiked into
a pattern of death.
Tall fir and maple,
snags
twenty feet off the trail,
alder in mid-descent
harried by time, sparse pale shoots
fringe a gnarl.

Shagged,
weary frames,

five storeys standing dead
in the south-to-north flyway.

Skunk cabbage
keeps the record
in elephantine ears
beneath elongated mosaics—
pilleated woodpecker's
knocking
in the hollow
ripe with termite.

5.
This evening the cat—
old Persian who sometimes
shuts down in general paralysis
—we take it
as reminiscence of a death—
scored himself two soft moles,
yodeling at the back door
to let us know he's back, in best health.

But his moles,
harvest of a soon-to-be abundance
given ample rain softens
the blind hotels
whence such rock stars emerge
to snap into jaws of adoring fans,
his moles
are morsels to this freak
I nearly fell on.

Dropped out of sky,
pelt smooth down hefty flanks,
the prong of his inch-long beak
calm and forgiving,
paws padded of a flesh
alike to the human God,
claws,
I can only approximate as fingers, up.

6.
Fingers plunged
through
cartilage of his own skull, Thomas à Kempis
awoke, entombed alive,
and, though scars
inside the coffin lid proved
he hoped for escape,
dug up by committee
for 17th century beatification,
he was assumed to have despaired
beneath the earth.

Oh, I'd rather be this little striver,
who, without a grunt of blame
or doubt an undeserved fate
ate up my existence, dug my way
through madness.
Did it never strike a mole
how much is lost
at the bottom
of the spectrum of aesthetic surmise?
Though something else goes awry
in the delicacy

of goldfinch
who hankers for sunlight
to accent an elegant plume,
this Apollo Mole, here under rain,
never conceived of ugliness,
not a seed of vanity for a moment,
and found other means
to quench the need to offspring.

Vanity is taught
perhaps to "show" animals
to incarnate our traits:
obedience, grace, usefulness,
rated by failure. Vanity in moles,
as in me, a lost cause, this spirit,
crisp fur rubbed with grit,
microbes already vainly try
to unstitch
in slime
and unclothe for the rain.

7.
When I squat
to study the bones,
I fall in
to my own inner life
of a blind varmint,
into my alien kidnap. Imagine:
probed lovingly by needle and talon,
hucked to the tips of old growth
above runnels out the swamp,
dams ditched when beaver
waddled out last spring

flooded to higher ground,
to a chew of cedar sapling,
initiate in the climax,
and upward in the arc I am clutched
above my own tracks
fringed along the fairway
of charred slash, industrial debris
and dropped here, face up, corrupt,
blinded by the body of the Bear
through the chaos of freezing Orion,
dropped where I sing this,
my mouth stuffed with dirt,
till your soft hands roll me over,
forepaws crimp inward, and I
begin to dig. How am I not
the luckiest mole?

Michael Daley, born and raised in Dorchester, Massachusetts, entered religious life at a young age, but by 20 was wild in the streets, protesting wars and seeking a life of experience. He traveled America hitchhiking, hopping freight trains, and working. He's been a waiter, a taxi driver, deckhand, tree-planter, laborer, impoverished journalist, small-press editor, Poet-in-the-Schools, and high school teacher. He's received awards from Seattle Arts Commission, Artist Trust, Fulbright, and National Endowment of the Humanities. He lives with his wife, Kathy Prunty, in Anacortes, Washington.

Books from *Empty Bowl*, a division of Pleasure Boat Studio

Glenolden Park   Richard Lloyd
Hanoi Rhapsodies   Scott Ezell
P'u Ming's Oxherding Pictures & Verses
    trans. from Chinese by Red Pine
Swimming the Colorado   Denise Banker
Lessons Learned   Finn Wilcox
Petroglyph, Americana   Scott Ezell
Old Tale Road   Andrew Schelling
Working the Woods, Working the Sea
    Eds. Finn Wilcox, Jerry Gorsline
The Blossoms Are Ghosts at the Wedding
Tom Jay with essays
Desire Jody   Aliesan
Dreams of the Hand   Susan Goldwitz
The Basin: Poems from a Chinese Province   Mike O'Connor
The Straits   Michael Daley
In Our Hearts and Minds: The Northwest and Central America
    ed. Michael Daley
The Rainshadow   Mike O'Connor
Untold Stories   William Slaughter

Pleasure Boat Studio books are available by order from your
bookstore, directly from our website, or through the following:

SPD (Small Press Distribution)
Tel. 800-869-7553, Fax 510-524-0852

Partners/West
Tel. 425-227-8486, Fax 425-204-2448

Baker & Taylor
Tel. 800-775-1100, Fax 800-775-7480

Ingram
Tel. 615-793-5000, Fax 615-287-5429

Amazon.com or Barnesandnoble.com